The Art of Being

Alexandra Bogdanovic

BookLeaf
Publishing

Presentation by *BookLeaf Publishing*

Web: www.bookleafpub.com

E-mail: info@bookleafpub.com

ISBN: 9789357212939

First edition 2023

*To Ruby, Lola and all our adventures of 2022 -
OMG!*

ACKNOWLEDGEMENT

My eternal thanks to Ruby, Lola and all my family and friends for the gift of unconditional love, every step on the way, always and forever.

And my heartfelt thank YOU for reading my poems. They are yours, now.

PREFACE

The Art of Being has one guiding principle: choose you thoughts and your words as you choose you clothes, and your world will rearrange according to your desires.

What goes around, comes around. Be brave. Be bold. Be yourself.

Your Life

It could be as little
or as big as you wish,
someday you are a shark
other day you are a small golden fish.

You burn through the fires of love and pain alike
and only with hindsight you can understand
that each moment and each path
for you – was right.

Your journey could be a walk in the park,
a gentle hike or a tumble down the rabbit hole,
yet always leading to some amazing chances,
if you remember to look beyond and above the
illusionary wall.

Embrace your dreams and go with that flow,
play, fly and soar beyond what you know,
you are here for a brief drop of time,
swing through your life like a good luck wind
chime.

Freedom

Let your heart choose your path.
Forget about 'maybe', do not do 'perhaps'
Only go for the 'Hell, yes!'
and watch the melt down of all your mess.

Your days are meant for being,
your nights are here for you to rest.
The only real job is to breathe,
the rest is smoke and mirrors, do not get
impressed.

Those who love you will glow with you,
without blame, without fear, with a spark,
And when your heart is in the right place,
you can trust the path ahead,
even when it gets foggy, gloomy and dark

Paris at Night

The lights are white and bright
like snowy peaks in the Alps
reflecting the glitter of summits and dunes,
and hopes of the transiting Moons.

We long to Zing, so we try and we pass,
until the chains of connections click,
then we just close our eyes and smile
knowing the bliss of an arrested time blink.

Living by the Sea

Your know the drill
and how life goes.

There are days that promise nothing
yet they burst with piercing morning sunshine
into your eyes
until the little light from within
starts to flicker.

And it flickers until it triggers something
you didn't even know was there.
Or you maybe just forgot about it.

So you suddenly, as if by magic,
you recognise, remember and know
how extraordinary it is to be alive and here,

And what a miracle you must be
to be able to smell, hear and see
the autumn air, sounds and colours
by the sea.

Despacito

I remember the day I saw you first,
wondering if you were a vision visiting the
earth...
I was in so much awe and so star-struck
that I didn't think that you were real,
you were more a dream-like.

I said to all who would listen then
that I have met someone from beyond the realm,
and even though I didn't dare to look you in the
eye
my mind was crystal clear, as a blue summer
sky.

It was only the matter of time
that our two paths would cross,
for us to stop and smile,
and allow the words to gloss.

When the mid-summer night sat us together,
the ground opened, and what a sway!
From that moment there was nothing on the
planet
that could keep us apart and away.

When you know it and don't know it

We are the match
and the time is now
even though I cannot see what,
where and how.

Out of the blue
with few small cute words
you've unlocked the invisible door between the
worlds
and I started to hear the songs of the birds.

If it isn't right, they said, go left,
whatever that might be in your mind.
The options are limitless,
just stay on course of love and remain kind.

Doubt and fear, my dear

You said that we met
and that nothing can stand on our path.
We will work it out.
Everything.
Whatever
However.
Wherever.
But what if we get stopped in time,
and just have that, what we already had?
And what if our dreams and plans
remain buried in the words already spoken, and
unspoken?
What if we stay burning in the fires already
gone?
What if all we ever get
are the precious few little moments that we've
already shared?
What if the act of finding
and knowing that there is a match,
your match,
is the top prize?
What if Life decides to keep us apart?
What then.

In your eyes

Never before
I knew so clearly and so fully
that life is right
that all is well
in my bones,
in my blood
in my head
the world has shrunk
and then exploded
like a mirror
cracked in a million pieces.
Somehow
the burst has found me still and solid.
There wasn't hope,
no pain, no pleasure,
just some light presence in each of the million
moments
happening all together
with a promise and premise of eternity
with you.

Jane

I met Jane on the train.

The day was bleak with a misty rain;
December cold froze the bones from the inside,
Jane wore a hat and when she looked at me
the ambience changed, as if the Sun shone from
the outside.

We talked of many things
real and some less so,
most of this plain,
few from beyond the main,
And between the words unspoken
and the things we said,
our souls embraced
and we flew to Neverland.

I could see us catching up in our two cottages in
the woods
for many years to come.
I felt the joy of the promise of a friendship new,
it was as loud as a beating drum.

There was a clear moment in time to pin
when I recognised the vibe:

I knew that Jane from the train was my friend
and that I was one of her tribe.

From beyond

What if
I have already
passed over
and
it is just my spirit
wondering
down the old corridors
of unfinished businesses,
hanging out to facilitate
the closures
for others
who remain stuck in the old stories
of errors and blame?

What if I am already elsewhere
on my journey to the next place,
but have opted for my soul
to stay for few moments longer
to offer
the last drop of love,
forgiveness and kindness
to those
I loved,
and left?

Pray

Pray
to know how to focus on love
that shines in us all,
pray to know that all is well,
when you are in the middle of a raging storm.

Pray to be able and willing to forgive
even as the sharp pain pierce your soul,
Pray to remember how to smile
even when all is lost in the sea of sadness and its
black hole.

Pray to know how to deal
with the reflections you see as cold and evil,
Pray for the inspired actions and stories
that lift you towards a creative upheaval.

Walking with the Stars

I went on a walkabout
with the stars last night
and we had a little conversation
about all the things that weren't right.

The crockery and cutlery in my head,
and all the rules that no longer worked,
the 'musts' and 'shoulds' and 'woulds'
stepped out to play, in a noisy way.

By the time the Mummy-star appeared
to take my stars to sleep,
I've been freed from my old rule-books all
together,
and I felt light as a feather.

The Masterclass

The time has come for a master-class
on how to hold your grounds
and how to keep the smile on your face
whatever the outward rounds.

When the reality offers you lectures
in the form of words, feels and actions
that aren't kind
stop for a breather,
close eyes for a moment
and let them wash-over your mind.

Allow the kicks to lead and land you
where you'd most like to be,
say your thanks to whatever it is,
shift the horizon,
and allow your daydream to be all you see.

You stay in sync with love and your values
regardless of the noises from the outside,
you know it better, you know for sure,
that your path is only dictated by that precious
flame from the inside

Sun-rise

As I stood and watched
the Sun rise over the ocean yesterday,
with the full Moon still beaming behind me,
I saw the ocean sway and hug the sky,
and how to sky melted into the watery horizon,
swapping the colours of rainbow,
in the rhythm of
the distant stars twinkling,
as if in silent approval of it all.
And I smiled admiring their play,
allowing
all my worries to melt away.

Love for life

Not all the mornings are sunny
and not every sunset is gold.
Not every word you hear is kind,
and not everyone you meet is brave and bold.

Some days may be cold and cloudy,
and there will be sleepless nights.
Some people will shout and thunder and lie
and sometime you will not know why.

There may be moments of sadness
when tears will wash out your eyes
but all is worth, all is precious,
you stay yourself, do enjoy and love your life.

Walk your path

You cannot do it others
regardless of all the love and care,
We each walk our own path to light
the best we can, whatever the glare.

The signs are around each single step,
do not worry about the aftermath,
just stay determined to be yourself
and firmly stay on your path.

Hope

You have no hope in the world,
they said

Actually,
I have all the hope in the world.

In fact,
I have nothing else
but hope and faith
that
Love will prevail.

I know it in my bones.
I know it in the hearts of my heart:
Love will prevail.

What goes around,
comes around.

Love

Like the Source itself,

I am still feeling every word,
every emotion
and every note
of everything you ever wrote,

Yet
I am choosing to stay away,
choosing to be invisible,
choosing not to say a thing,
I am choosing silence.

Because
I know how precious
the moments have been
and how nothing ended
at the end.

We just allowed Life
to take us further
from that moment
from that smile
from the promise
of us
forever.

And when you know it,
you know it.

The Dream of Thinking

21

To stay in the flow
is all you wish to know
Yet there is a voice
asking you to go:

To break the mould,
to create some art
and smash the rules and random choices
that suppose to be smart.

The crunch time is coming closer
you shall hear the news to set you free
and then you'll see what's truly possible
and what and how else your life could be.

A call

You
who know how little time we have
and who would not want to miss
any precious moment together.

You
who feel in your bones
that there is me out there
wondering how this beautiful world
continues to spin without us.

You
who can hear the sweet vibrations of my longing
for home and family,
you know,
for real, with you.

You,
out-there, walking the days alone, in circles,
turning the moments into questions,
you, speak up and answer.

Love is a bridge

Love is a bridge
from the land of impossible and unlikely
to the land of everything is possible.

Love is a bridge
from the town of tiredness and gloom
to the city of being wide-awake,
of curiosity and joy.

Even when it hurts,
Love is a bridge
between the islands of pain and despair
and the isles of hope and prayer.

Love is the bridge
between you and you, when you get it right,
and when it finds you,
there is nothing that can stop you from walking
across.

Love is your bridge.

www.ingramcontent.com/pod-product-compliance
Lightning Source LLC
Chambersburg PA
CBHW070731160726
48003CB00006BA/2449